PLASS WITH  ATTITUDE

Andrew Fusek Peters &
Polly Peters

angelcake

HODDER
Wayland

An imprint of Hodder Children's Books

Text copyright © Andrew Fusek Peters and Polly Peters 2001

First published in Great Britain in 2001 by Hodder Wayland,
an imprint of Hodder Children's Books.

10 9 8 7 6 5 4 3 2 1

British Library Cataloguing in Publication Data

Peters, Andrew, 1962-
Angelcake. - (Plays with Attitude)
1. AIDS (Disease) 2. Children's plays, English
I. Title II. Peters, Polly
822.9'14

ISBN 0 7502 3458 X

Printed in Hong Kong by Wing King Tong

Hodder Children's Books
A division of Hodder Headline Limited
338 Euston Road, London NW1 3BH

FOREWORD

Death and sex: the two things without which life cannot exist. But what happens when one leads directly to the other? Set in the early 1990s, before the advent of anti-retroviral drugs in the West, *Angelcake* deals with the issues of HIV, AIDS and STDs. The play explores the themes of bereavement, family relationships and consequences.

The plot follows the unfolding story of siblings Leah and David. Structured through the device of Leah's journal, it chronicles David's contraction of the HIV virus and his and Leah's subsequent journey through life and death. This narrative is combined with chorally dramatised sections of poetry which express both outward and inner responses to the situation. There is a mix of light and dark humour with the ultimate bleakness of loss and a range of emotional responses. The emphasis throughout is that this can happen to anyone; also that grief is something which affects everyone at some time and that the only way forward is to face and feel it. If there is a moral, it is about making informed choices and about taking personal responsibility.

The cast size required for *Angelcake* is deliberately flexible so that it can be performed by drama groups of different sizes. It can be performed with a minimum cast of 10 (with creative doubling and a small chorus) or can accommodate 30 to 40 performers with a large chorus or with several different chorus groups. There is scope for a lot of group-based ensemble work.

Angelcake contrasts the realism of the character-based scenes with the stylisation of the physically and vocally choreographed chorus sequences. These atmospheric chorus sections are intended to allow for extensive creative and dramatic exploration and interpretation during rehearsal or lessons – certain sections could be set to dance. The character of Leah acts as narrator through the use of journal-based monologue, though this is open to inventive re-interpretation for a small group to participate in this narration.

Angelcake is suitable for Key Stage 4 (aged 15+) and Sixth Form.

CAST LIST

LEAH

DAVID   Leah's brother

BEE   David's girlfriend

MARK   David's mate

JO   Leah's friend

ELAINE   Leah's friend

DANIELLA   Leah's friend

GIRLFRIENDS David's four ex-girlfriends (non-speaking)

MUM   Leah's and David's mum

DAD   Leah's and David's dad

NARRATOR(S)

SECRETARY

HEALTH ADVISER

TEACHER

CHORUS   Text often specifies ten performers as chorus.
             However, chorus size is intended to be entirely
             flexible to accommodate small or large groups.
             Stage directions for chorus are minimal to allow
             for directorial interpretation of these scenes.

4

Scene 1

Chairs and small, lightweight tables suggest a café. CHORUS, *as cafégoers, hold frozen, silent poses during* LEAH'*s opening speech.* LEAH *is seated alone.*

LEAH, *writing in her journal:*

> 23 April 1992: I live in Dull House, on Blink-And-You-Miss-It Street in the town of Wherever-You-Fancy. My dad isn't a drunk and Mum doesn't scream at me, so I guess we get on fairly well. My brother David's a different story: aged aunts with zipped lips were most upset when he left school, then home to follow his first love. And I'm not writing about girls – though he is an utter flirt – but food. Yeah, that was his adolescent rebellion against years of TV dinners squirming about on our laps like some ancient endangered species. The other lads at school jeered, but home economics was the making of our David. Most of them are stacking shelves now, while my brother is building stacks of passionfruit pancakes. He's shown them – started off wiping tables and now he's running the place. No Greasy Joe either – but fry-ups with attitude. He's considered a bit of a dish himself and so is what he serves. And me? Stacks of

imagination. Anything to escape our dull life. At school I'm no swot, but nor am I sniffing glue behind the science block. This is my story. About David. About my family and about everyone.

Café scene comes to life around her – one chorus member brings a cup of tea, tables fill up with chat and laughter. School friends enter and crowd around LEAH's *table.*

LEAH: All right, everyone? What do you think then? [*Indicates café*]

ELAINE: Not bad, not bad at all. Even smells edible. We're staying.

DANIELLA: So, give us the grease, Leah.

JO: We demand zit development rights.

LEAH: Yeah right. Just one taste of my brother's cooking will melt your hearts. Trust me!

ELAINE: Well, I've heard he's something in the lurve department.

LEAH: You are obsessed and very sad, Elaine.

DANIELLA: Well, where is David then? Haven't seen him since he was in school uniform.

ELAINE: I like a man in uniform.

LEAH: David, in school clothes? Don't think he ever bothered.

JO: He had a tie, always covered in his latest recipes. I used to watch him.

ELAINE: Yeah?

JO: Yeah, but we were little baby Year 8s. Never gave
            us a second glance.

DAVID *approaches.*

DAVID: [*Affectionate to* LEAH] Leah, why are your friends
            so gorgeous? Aren't you going to introduce us?

LEAH: Oh, God, here we go!

DAVID: Don't worry, little sis – I'm not a total chauvinist
            pig. I just serve up their little trotters!

ELAINE: Yeurgh!

DAVID: Don't worry – I do sense that offal would not go
            down 'offally' well. [*Girls groan*] But we do a
            fantastic home-made pizza – peppers roasted in
            extra virgins…

JO: What?

DAVID: Sorry, extra virgin olive oil, with capers, anchovies,
            cheese so stringy you could wrap parcels with it.
            What do you think?

ALL: Mmmmm!

DAVID: Right! [*Takes order, then moves away*]

JO: I have just died and gone to heaven. He's drop
            dead… and a dab hand with nibbles. Is he seeing
            anyone?

LEAH: Do you mind? I thought you lot came to see me.
            Or did you? Hmmm.

All except LEAH *freeze.* LEAH *spotlit with journal.*

LEAH, *writing in journal*:

> That was his way with words, the chat-up followed by the fry-up, followed by the... need I say more? This guy can count the number of his girlfriends on the fingers of a millipede! Let's see which ones I can actually remember...

All move chairs into two vertical lines, facing each other to provide a catwalk down the middle. LEAH *continues writing and is the last to move.*

NARRATOR: Girlfriend number one is a bit of rough.

> [GIRLFRIEND 1 *stomps onstage*] She is wearing this season's frayed jacket with strategic rips and a matching handbag with spikes on the outside. She doesn't need a stud. She's covered in them.

Applause from seated CHORUS *who mime taking photos.*

NARRATOR: Girlfriend number two [GIRLFRIEND 2 *comes onstage*] sports the current anorexic look. She is wearing the latest see-through-to-the-bone combination, with a cross-my-heart-and-hope-to-diet bra. Jaunty as a near-death experience, with a boyfriend who tried feeding her up and is now fed up... Moving on now before we get too bored... [GIRLFRIEND 3 *comes onstage*] Girlfriend number seven is in the army. She likes David to stand to attention, but he thinks she's a bit of an obstacle course. After a night out clubbing, she went AWOL and is currently missing

in action. [GIRLFRIEND 4 comes onstage] Girlfriend
number 260 – I'm not exaggerating, honest guv, all
the lads do it. Anyway, what's a few added zeros
between friends when you've been down the pub
– is tall and willowy with the buddy beautiful. She
has dear David rooted to the spot. He twigged
that she's barking. She told him to 'leaf her alone'.

CHORUS *groan, then clap. Fourth girlfriend exits. All freeze
except* LEAH, *spotlit.*

LEAH, *writing in journal*:

> And on and on and on. He collected girlfriends like
> stamps. Mum and Dad always tried to remember
> their names as they shook endless pairs of hands. It
> wasn't that he was a one-night-stand sort of boy.
> His passion flamed like that gas cooker of his – the
> great heat in the middle of a fantastic concoction –
> but when pudding was done, lips smacked in
> delight and wiped, the bill paid, the café grew
> suddenly empty. Bless him, he always thought the
> next one would be it. And she was.

*Sound of music as all move chairs back around tables, then
mime sitting at a club.* DAVID *and* MARK *spotlit. Music fades.*

DAVID: And there she was, in the club. I'd just knocked off
             for the night and was desperate for a vol-au-vent-
             free zone.

MARK: I'm all ears, my old chump chop. Did you try the 'come-and-see-my-designer-flat-above-the-groovy-café-that-I-run' chat-up line? Not that I'm jealous, of course. In fact, shelf-stacking is a highly demanding position.

DAVID: I'm sure it is, Mark. Anyhow. For once, I was struck dumb. My brilliant cheesy chat-up went out the window. All I could say was the really original [*Loud music,* CHORUS *comes to life as clubbers*] 'Would you like a drink?'

CHORUS *members take over speech as* DAVID *mimes actions with girlfriend,* BEE.

1: And the next moment

2: She was serving up

3: Her whole life story on a plate.

4: That was it. David's fate

5: Was sealed.

6: The apple of lurve was peeled.

7: She told him, her old flame had been up to his old tricks

8: Dropped her, preferred his fix,

9: In love with the drug.

10: Well, she wasn't a total mug,

1: Got the hell out of there

2: And now she was alone

3: As if anyone cares.

4:	Full of emotions stewing away
5:	So why did David take her away?
6:	She was gorgeous, sensitive, drop dead
7:	'Nuff said.
8:	Back to the caff
9:	Bit of a laff:
10:	One thing led
1:	To the upstairs bed! [BEE and DAVID exit]
8:	Their love was passionate
9:	Who needs protection?
10:	Raincoats are for wimps
1:	A sensual rejection.

Club scenes freezes. DAVID *re-enters.*

MARK:	Sounds well dodgy to me!
DAVID:	Thanks Mark, you're a mate. You've just got to understand that I am—
MARK:	Nuts!
1:	Head over heels
2:	Besotted
3:	Doolally
4:	Bonkers
5:	It's lust
6:	Or bust!
5:	You get the picture
6:	Love is blind
7:	Our David is out of his mind!

CHORUS *freeze.*

DAVID: I tell you, Mark, the first time it feels real and she's gone and moved away. Her dad got some job up North. It's not fair. I'd only been seeing her for a couple of months, and the last bit of that I was laid up in bed with the flu.

MARK: Poor you!

DAVID: I haven't seen her for four weeks, what with the café and her getting settled in – it's an eight-hour drive on the damn motorway.

MARK: What's eight hours between friends?

DAVID: Too much, I tell you. Anyhow, she's coming down this weekend and I'm pulling out all the stops. Gourmet or not gourmet...

MARK: ... That is the question. The road of lust is paved with good cooks, or something like that. Anyhow, she must be missing that bed of yours. You are so tacky, David.

DAVID: Someone has to have a strawberry-shaped bed! Anyhow, she's doing my head in. The other day, I served someone a napkin on a plate... with a sprig of parsley on it for God's sake!

MARK: You are a sad goner. Your head is scrambled, mate. [*He moves away*]

DAVID: Egg-zactly!

DAVID *freezes.*

CHORUS *step forward to act out* DAVID*'s inner poetic thoughts through choreographed movement with background music.*

DAVID: In the club, that night, we danced

1:          Locked together like salt and vinegar,

2:          Rhythm whisked up to a froth

3:          Dark recipes followed with

ALL: Zest

4:          In the shadows.

5:          All words are sudden spices,

            The flavour of flirting is strong.

CHORUS *repeat and enact improvised chat-up lines.*

6:          You are hot pepper

7:          And your kisses burn my tongue,

8:          Leaving the taste of love lingering

9:          Long

10:         Long

DAVID: Long in the moon yolk of night

            After you have gone.

CHORUS: [*Echoing words*] Gone, gone, gone… [*Fade, sit
            back down at tables as though in café*]

Scene 2

Café scene comes to life again. Bee *walks in.* David *sees her, rushes up to kiss her. She turns her cheek. Background chatter continues, clattering knives etc.*

DAVID: Bee?

BEE: David. This is too busy. Can we go upstairs?

DAVID: Oh, blimey, you don't hang around. I mean, yes, please. [*He signals to a waiter to carry on without him*]

David *and* Bee *move off to side of stage.* Chorus *remain static in café positions.*

DAVID: How my kitschy bed, my divine strawberry in sheets has missed you! [*Lunges towards her. She pushes him off.*] Hey? Sorry… just missed touching you.

BEE: I can't stay.

DAVID: What do you mean? You've just got here. I've missed you, Bee. My recipes seem sad without you.

BEE: Just listen will you? I need to tell you… I…
           My ex-boyfriend has been in touch.

DAVID: So? What? Mr Off-his-head? I hope you told him that you're with someone else, now – me!

BEE: There's something else.

DAVID: What? He's not trying to get back with you, is he?

You're not...?

BEE: He's been in touch with every girlfriend he ever slept with.

DAVID: What a sad git. He must be desperate.

BEE: Listen will you? This is really hard for me. He told me. He told me that... he told me that he's HIV positive. OK?

DAVID: What? I don't understand.

BEE: Sharing needles. 'Unprotected sex.' Do I have to spell it out, David?

DAVID: Bee?

BEE: Don't touch me. Don't ever touch me again. Bloody boys. You're all the same. 'It feels more natural without any protection', eh? Well I wasn't pro-tected. A little daily pill can't stop what I've got.

DAVID: But that means that you... I might... Oh, Christ.

BEE: I can't cope with this. I've told you. That's what I came here to do. I owe you that. Face to face. Oh, David... what you do now is up to you. I'm going. I can't see you, I don't want to see you. Don't try to contact me, ever. I don't want to know. [*She exits 'downstairs'*]

DAVID: [*Standing up*] Bee! Bee!

He runs 'downstairs' to the café, devastated. He sits down at empty table. CHORUS *start coughing, whispering the word* HIV *under their breath.*

LEAH: All right, David? [DAVID *says nothing*] Hey, Mr Earplug, didn't you hear me?

DAVID: Yes. Haven't you got anywhere better to go?

LEAH: I always come here after school. Cup of tea for a starving swot?

DAVID: Who do you think I am? Your sodding slave? Jesus, what with you and that stupid diary and your girly, giggly, slapper friends, crowding out my café and giving me lung cancer and not spending any money… This is a business, not a teenage drop-in centre. So, go drop out somewhere else.

LEAH: Hang on, David. What brought this on? [DAVID *walks off without looking at her*] David?

LEAH *exits in opposite direction.*

Scene 3

CHORUS *use text for physical theatre ensemble performance. They have set movements for each line.* DAVID *and* BEE *enter to act with* CHORUS. *Music. Two* NARRATORS, *boy and girl stand on opposite sides of stage, frozen, apart from voices.*

BOY: Under the vaulted sky [*Arms up as if in prayer*]
Whisper a thousand conspiracies,
[CHORUS *mutter Chinese whispers around stage*]

GIRL:	Our love was one of them.
BOY:	I held you like banknotes,
BOTH:	Ran my silver thread right through you. [*Hold up an imaginary banknote to look for thread*]
BOY:	In the pale morning light I paid the price.
CHORUS:	[*Echoing*] How much? How much? [*Answering*] Too much, Too much.
GIRL:	Our numbers added up [*Chorus writing figures*]
BOTH:	Big sums, the profit of passion [*Thumbs up, swivelling hips*]
BOY:	And then we crashed, [*Sudden collapse at the knees*]
GIRL:	The system went down, [*Further collapse*]
BOY:	Corrupted by a
ALL:	Virus
GIRL:	The world tilting sideways

All bend on one knee and sway to one side.

BOY:	Throwing your past into my hands [*Makes movement as if throwing upwards*] Like bent gold sovereigns.

All still bent over, backing away to edges of stage, lining up with narrators, facing away to freeze. Music fades.

Scene 4

LEAH, *writing in journal*:

22 June 1992: What brought this on? I know the job is hard, but my brother is a trooper. 'Sleep is for limp lettuces,' he always says. And what did I do? Oh, I get it. His girlfriend chucks him and he takes it all out on little sis. It's always been the way. Next girlfriend he gets, he'll confide in me all about it, but now he's down in the dumps, and I'm in the way. What a prize git. Let him stew. I'm not waiting around this time. [*Exits*]

Scene 5

DAVID *enters walking up and down empty café. Some punters try to open door.* CHORUS *lift up sign saying Closed.* DAVID *points at sign and carries on pacing.*

1:	But David is waiting
2:	And waiting
3:	And waiting
4:	He's had the test
5:	And his head can't rest
6:	Till he knows

7:      Whether the virus is passed

8:      Like dominoes

9:      From smackhead

10:     To hop into bed

1:      From darling buzz of a Bee

2:      To David.

3:      It's mad

4:      It's a mystery

5:      This tracing of sexual history.

CHORUS *mime men in suits, lounging with hands in pockets, walking in choreographed motions. There is the notion of time passing, through* CHORUS *movement, the use of clock sound effects, or diary flipping by* DAVID *as he stands anxiously at the side of the stage.*

6:      These are the silent days.

        Men are walking slowly by,

        Departing in trains,

7:      Arriving at destinations,

        Leaning on iron railings.

8:      These are the silent days.

        The silence of laughter

        Moving through the ribcage

        Of the mind,

9:      So many faces,

        Too many faces,

        The laugh is in all of them...

10: Here being the silent days

Where gods are walking

With hands in their pockets,

Too idle to dice,

Too slow to make miracles,

Too dull to care...

The cards are falling

ALL: Randomly.

1: These are the silent days.

Scene 6

DAVID *steps forward.* CHORUS *move tables and chairs to suggest a waiting room and a consulting room, then physically form a door shape between.* HEALTH ADVISER *sits.*

SECRETARY: David Symonds? David Symonds, please.

DAVID: Oh. That's me.

SECRETARY: The health adviser is ready to see you now.

DAVID *goes through 'door'.*

HEALTH ADVISER: Have a seat, David.

DAVID: Thanks. [*Sits*]

HEALTH ADVISER: The last time I saw you for pre-test counselling, we tried to work out when you last put yourself at risk. It can take three months for the HIV antibodies to reach detectable levels. That's why we sometimes offer a second test if a client has had unprotected sex more recently.

DAVID: Well, I had the flu, and then she moved – so… it's been three months. God that sounds sad for someone my age. [*Laughs nervously*] But waiting these two weeks has been terrible.

HEALTH ADVISER: I do understand, and I am very sorry David. The results are positive.

DAVID: But if it's positive, that's good isn't it?

HEALTH ADVISER: The language of these things is a mess. You have tested positively, which means that we've found antibodies to the HIV virus. That means you are HIV positive.

DAVID: Wow. Yeah. God. Oh, God. I'm too young for this. [HEALTH ADVISER *passes him paper hankie*] It doesn't seem possible. I fall in love, and it's going to kill me.

HEALTH ADVISER: This is a shock, but there is a lot of help available and we can start talking about counselling and treatment options. The important thing is that you are healthy right now. Also, because you came to the STD clinic, these results are totally confidential and won't appear on your medical record. Don't be alone in this David.

DAVID: Thanks. Well… I'd better be going.

DAVID *shakes* HEALTH ADVISER'*s hand. Both exit. Lights fade.*

Scene 7

Lights up. DAVID *and* LEAH *are on stage.* DAVID *is slowly setting up café.*

DAVID: Hey, Leah, give me a hand putting these straight, will you? Look, I'm sorry about how I've been and I'm glad to see you here again. It's been a while.

LEAH: Yeah? Four weeks…

Pause, while chair and table-moving is completed. LEAH *watches* DAVID, *who is absorbed.*

DAVID: There! Right. I've got home-cured bacon, free-range eggs, tomatoes grilled in basil and olive oil and mushrooms to die for.

LEAH: [*The tension is broken*] God, you win me over so easily. What is it this time? Not another girlfriend already? No, don't tell me, your ex was a serial murderess and you've been questioned by the police.

DAVID: I'm questioning everything, Leah. I can't believe what's happened.

LEAH: You mean, she dumped you? Get over it. So, she wasn't your type.

DAVID: I won't ever get over it.

LEAH: Don't be such a drama queen.

DAVID: Leah, just listen to me. I got this flu thing a couple of months ago, just after I started seeing Bee. I didn't know that that was one of the first symptoms. Then Bee came here and told me about her ex-boyfriend. That he had it…

LEAH: Had what?

David: [*Continues as if she hasn't spoken*] Of course, in the heat of the moment, we never worried about protection. It didn't seem possible, but now I've had the test.

LEAH: Where's this going, David? What are you talking about?

DAVID: I've got HIV. Bee and I had unprotected sex. At least I remember *that* from school. Like a daisy chain, he gave it to Bee and Bee gave it to me. I'm truly shagged this time.

LEAH: [*Gobsmacked*] This is… you're… I can't. You're only 19. You're joking. [DAVID *shakes head*] But I thought that…

DAVID: I've been doing a lot of thinking. I don't know what happens now.

DAVID *walks off*. LEAH *takes out journal*.

LEAH, *writing in journal*:

> 22 July, 1992. I don't understand… it seems impossible, my full-of-life brother sentenced to death. I've heard there are all sorts of drugs, but no cure. Christ. No cure… All for one bloody moment of passion. But who am I to judge? I've been close to it with Matt for ages – and some nights I just want to give in to his wandering hands, go all the way. My mates reckon I'm living in medieval times. Elaine thinks she's so sodding clever by squawking 'Get thee to a nunnery!' every time we go clubbing. I bet she fancies Matt… The thing is, I'm just not ready yet, though maybe Matt won't hang around for ever, and maybe Elaine's right – what's the big deal? Just because half my class are at it – or say they're at it more likely – doesn't mean I have to go with the crowd. I'm not prim or proper or particularly religious. I just want to make my own mind up, know that it's my decision, not theirs. Oh, David. What's going to happen to my brother now? [LEAH *continues writing in journal*]

CHORUS *enter and choreograph poem, with set movements for each line and a repeated movement for the first line of each verse.*

ALL: For when my brother dies

1:          I shall cry tears of stone

Never will I have felt so alone

And my heart will try to be hard.

ALL: For when my brother dies

2:         No more late-night Monopoly and after

Bacon and eggs with a cup of laughter

The yolk of dawn just breaking.

ALL: For when my brother dies

3:         I shall cry a city of tears

Then put on a smile, hide all my fears

If only I could, if only…

ALL: For when my brother dies

5:         I shall cry blades of grass

People will be polite, dare not ask

Why my garden overgrows.

ALL: For when my brother dies

6:         I shall have no brother

No other to hug and to hold

CHORUS *freeze*.

LEAH: [*Looking up from journal*] And I the younger,

am the one who will grow old.

CHORUS *come to life to fill up café.* LEAH*'s mates enter and join* LEAH.

ELAINE:	All right, Leah? I think you're more in love with that diary of yours than Matt Splatt.
LEAH:	He's not that spotty.
DANIELLA:	Let's just say they've started mountaineering courses round his chin!
LEAH:	Oh, you're *so* funny.
JO:	You seem a bit quiet today. Everything OK?
LEAH:	Well…
ELAINE:	And where is that brother of yours? I'm desperate for some 'service'. Hey David! [*She sees him offstage*]
DAVID:	Yeah?
ELAINE:	What, no cheesy chat-ups today?
DAVID:	No. What do you want?
ELAINE:	Oh. Er. Right. Cup of tea.
DANIELLA:	Me too.
JO:	And me. [DAVID *walks off*] He looks like he's seen a ghost.
LEAH:	He has.
JO:	What?
LEAH:	Nothing. [*She gets up and goes to speak to* DAVID *at side of stage. Member of* CHORUS *takes teas over to table*] Easy does it, David.

DAVID: I can't handle it, Leah. I've got this thing about knives. Every time I chop a vegetable, I wonder if I'm gonna chop too far and cut myself. My blood is full of this crap. This virus, thanks to, thanks to… well, thanks to me, actually… Would that be a little grilled HIV with your potatoes, sir?

LEAH: [*Holding him*] Calm down. Hey…

DAVID: I've lost my love and now I've lost my living. I can't cook. I can't. Cooking is creative. This is destroying me.

LEAH: Get someone else to do all that chopping stuff. Run the place. Do the menus. How can a recipe harm anyone? You can't give up this easily.

DAVID: Yeah. Yeah. You're right, sis. Do you…? Do you still love me?

LEAH: Don't know why, but I do.

DAVID: I'm so stupid. If only I'd thought… Look Leah, if Matt ever gets his wicked way with you, make sure he uses a condom, right?

LEAH: I'm not thinking about Matt much at the moment, but believe me, I get the message. Now stop blaming yourself. There's no point. Do your job. You're good at it.

DAVID: Yeah. Right.

LEAH *goes back to the table.*

ELAINE: What was that all about? He doesn't lurve me any more…

LEAH: He never did, Elaine.

JO: He was a bit off.

DANIELLA: Yeah, like the food today.

LEAH: It's the job, you know. He's under a lot of pressure

ELAINE: I'd like to be under his pressure!

All groan and drink up.

JO: You coming, Leah?

LEAH: No, gonna catch up with my writing.

ELAINE: [*As she walks off*] She definitely loves that diary more than her so-called boyfriend.

DANIELLA *carries cups offstage on tray. All exit.*

Scene 8

LEAH, *writing in journal*:

>1 November 1992: The leaves are full of fire today, but the wind is blowing them out. Winter's coming… David carried on for a while. Funny, but all that fear and frustration made fantastic food. The menus got wild and the café was packed.

DAVID *and* CHORUS *mime actions.*

1:          David carried on the dance

2:          Even managed to entrance

3:          A few girls that wafted in the door.

4:          But it was never more

5:          Than that.

6:          Food and flirting were as far as it went

7:          And lonely nights were spent

8:          Tossing and turning with demons in his head

9:          And fear was the only food that fed

CHORUS *freeze.*

LEAH: His dark and tattered soul.

Blackout. CHORUS *exit.*

Scene 9

Lights up on LEAH, *sitting cross-legged on beanbag, to indicate home.*

LEAH, *writing in journal*:

> 23 April 1993: At home. The bluebells are out in the woods. I wanted to take my brother to see them, but he wasn't interested. A year since all this started. His T-cell count is down. Funny how school lessons are sometimes informative. The T-4 cells, bless 'em, are 'the immune system's key infection fighters'. The less he has, the more likely he is to start getting AIDS-related illnesses. Every time he gets a sniffle, my mum goes doolally with fear. He has less resistance than a baby. Last week, he had thrush, which I thought only girls got – but his was in his mouth – swelled up and everything, he could hardly speak. It was so heavy. This time, the antibiotics worked. I wish they'd hurry up and invent something to stop this freefall.

Leah *freezes.*

DAVID *enters, pacing.*

DAVID: [*manic*] Leave it, leave love, leave life, leave it alone.

CHORUS *enter and take over spoken lines. They are still, ranged around stage while* DAVID *runs up to them as they hold up and mime daffodils, colours, trees, girlfriends, sleep. He looks at each one for a second and then is repulsed by it.*

1:	Leave the dark sun leave daffodils leave colour
2:	Leave love leave it leave eyes leave touch
ALL:	Leave it, leave it, leave it all alone.
3:	Leave laughter leave trees leave leaves
4:	Leave nouns and meaning and leave sex
ALL:	Leave it, leave it, leave it all alone.
5:	Leave love leave love-making like rivers
6:	Leave diving in muddy waters leave dreams leave light
ALL:	Leave it, leave it, leave it all alone.
7:	Leave love leave love's sting leave it…
DAVID:	Leave it, leave it, leave it all alone [*He now slows down to a walk and then a shuffle and* CHORUS *take up narrative*]
8:	He's getting tired
9:	From the café retired
10:	It's no surprise
1:	The long days have left bags under his eyes.
2:	Immune system is shot
3:	And David is not
4:	Going to get well.

5:   A simple cold

All sneeze. DAVID *is buffeted by their sneezes and falls.*

6:   This too-young man

7:   Life's span cut short by snot

8:   It's not fair.

LEAH: [*Scribbling*] It's not fair. It's not fair. It's not bloody
     fair.

Blackout.

Scene 10

CHORUS *as pupils move tables and chairs into classroom layout
and sit down rowdily as pupils.*

TEACHER: When you are quite finished, as I was saying, the
     virus is passed through sharing needles, infected
     blood supplies and unprotected sexual intercourse.
     Kissing is totally safe.

ELAINE: Well, Leah's fine then, miss. She's only ever gone as
     far as a bit of tongue-in-cheek.

TEACHER: That's enough of your cheek. Believe it or not, this
     could easily affect you.

ELAINE: Oh, yeah. I'm not a smack addict or mates with any
     back-street boys!

BOY 1: Ho! Ho! Ho! Homo!

All laugh.

BOY 2: Look miss, I'm all right. It only gets queers and people in Africa. Why do we need to learn this?

ELAINE: Why not teach us different positions miss? That would be far more educational!

Shouts of Go Elaine! *and* You could teach her a thing or two!

ELAINE: [*Innocently*] What? I'm talking about yoga, of course. What did you think I meant?

All laugh.

BOY 3: This is boring. None of us is ever going to get HIV. Like he said, it's only the bender boys who need to watch out.

LEAH: [*Stands up*] Listen to you! The Nazis would've been proud. Your attitude disgusts me. This virus doesn't give a monkey's if you're straight, gay, male, female, on drugs or off drugs. It doesn't say, 'Oh look, there's someone with a lifestyle I don't approve of. I just think I'll wipe the lot of them out.'

TEACHER: Thank you, Leah. I was about to have a nervous breakdown and resign. And as for you [*Points to* BOY 3] I'll talk to you at the end of the lesson. Go on, Leah.

Calls of Teacher's Pet *and sucking noises from* CHORUS.

LEAH: [*To class*] You wanna play games! OK! Can I try something out on the class, miss?

TEACHER: Go ahead. Anything to get them to take this seriously.

LEAH: Let's see if your tiny brains can cope with this! Elaine. Stand up.

ELAINE: What is this? Leah, are you cracked or what?

LEAH: Do it.

ELAINE: All right then, Little Miss Virgin!

LEAH: [*Addressing class*] Elaine, let's for sake of this, call her Jane, thinks she's safe! She hasn't had that many partners. [*Class laughs*] Much. But let's just say, she's slept with two blokes.

ELAINE: Are you insulting my sex appeal or what?

LEAH: Can we have two blokes standing up? [*Laughter and jeers*] Let's just say those two blokes have slept with two girls each. Four girls stand up, please. Let's say that one of the girls was something of a goer, and slept with five blokes, and the others, one each. Eight blokes stand up please. And they've slept with two girls each apart from one, who hasn't had any luck yet.

CHORUS: Ahhhhh!

LEAH: 14 girls, please. That's more than the whole class… [*All standing looking silly*] The whole point is this, dear Elaine, sorry Jane! If any one single person in this room, anywhere along that chain of partners, had the virus, so could you by now. By sleeping with those two blokes, in terms of the virus, you might as well have slept with every person in this room. [*Embarrassed shuffling*] Think about it.

ELAINE: Yeah, well.

BOY 3: A waste of time, if you ask me.

TEACHER: We're not asking you, so be quiet and open your tiny brain for once.

Class cheers. Shouts of You said it, miss!

TEACHER: Thanks, Leah. That was very useful. And the point is, it's not just HIV, but sexually transmitted diseases like chlamydia. If your boyfriend isn't willing to use a condom and is carrying chlamydia, the infection you get could make you sterile. And where is the highest rate of infection? Teenagers. You lot.

Bell goes. CHORUS *as pupils make as if to rush out.*

TEACHER: Wait. I need some of you to help clear this room for the next lesson. And you [*To* BOY 3] can come with me.

CHORUS, *grumbling, remove tables and chairs.*

JO: [*Rushes up*] What's got into you, Leah? Elaine's a bit of wind-up, I know, but that was heavy.

ELAINE *comes forward.*

ELAINE: Well, you made me look a right pillock there.

LEAH: Good, you deserved it.

DANIELLA: She doesn't mean it, Leah.

LEAH: It's her attitude. Just something on the news. Nice and safe and far away. Won't ever come near to me. But it has. It's not just a lesson any more.

JO: What do you mean?

LEAH: What do I mean? I don't know. Don't know if I should even tell you.

DANIELLA: Not you? But that's impossible. Sexually transmitted right?

LEAH: Not me. No.

JO: What are you on about then?

LEAH: You really want to know? David's got it.

ELAINE: David? Your brother? Sex on legs?

LEAH: He was diagnosed. That's why he isn't at the café any more.

JO: Oh, God. Why didn't you tell us?

LEAH: Because I knew how you'd react. Now you know. Don't tell anyone. I couldn't handle the whole school knowing.

JO: Anything I can do, Leah. Anything.

DANIELLA: Me too.

ELAINE: And me, I suppose. [*Thinking, freaks out*] But, oh God, I drank cups of tea that he touched. Oh… Oh! That's disgusting. You should have told me. I don't believe it. I could have…

LEAH: [*Slapping her hard on the face*] You stupid, ignorant cow.

ELAINE: I didn't mean it.

LEAH *backs away.*

CHORUS *enter, miming actions to rest of scene.*

1:	The world divides
2:	Into whispered asides
3:	And those who are there
4:	Show they care.
5:	The ignorant filled with tabloid flaws
6:	Avoid her in the corridors.
7:	It's funny how your
ALL:	Friends
8:	React
9:	When face to face with the final act.
7:	Teachers offer sympathy
8:	And counsellors come with cups of tea.
9:	All that's asked is a little understanding
10:	It's not as if it's an alien landing.

CHORUS *disperse. Blackout.*

Scene 11

DAVID *is lying on beanbag, looking tired, watching TV.*
MARK *enters*

MARK: Hey Dave, long time no see. I went round the café and they said you'd come down with some bug. You're not infectious are you? I've brought the latest 'Alien' vid to cheer you up. You should see what it turns people into this time! We could get some bevvies in and become truly terrified!

DAVID: Not in the mood, mate.

MARK: Don't tell me, girlfriend trouble! I thought you were still seeing Bee? You're great at getting them, not so good at the keeping part. [*Sits down*]

DAVID: It's not a bug. It's HIV.

MARK: What? Like some weird strain of flu?

DAVID: My ex-girlfriend's boyfriend got it from sharing needles. He kindly gave it to her, and she unknowingly passed it on to me. HIV, Mark. It leads to AIDS.

MARK: AIDS. Are you...? Bloody hell.

DAVID: Hell is pretty close.

MARK: So, er... um... not in a movie mood then?

DAVID: No.

MARK: Right. I'm sorry. Don't know what to say. I can't get it by talking to you, can I?

DAVID: Don't be a jerk, Mark.

MARK: Right. Didn't think so. [*Shifts uncomfortably*]

DAVID: I went to see my uncle and aunt for the day. After I'd left, I found out that they sterilized every cup and plate and knife and sodding fork in the house. But the worst was, you know, the worst was that they wouldn't let me touch or cuddle my baby cousin. If you want aliens, you got it.

MARK: Sod 'em is all I can say. Well, I'm with you, mate. You're not dying yet, are you?

DAVID: No, just very tired. Very effing tired. I miss the café and the banter and my girlfriend... oh, yeah... ex-girlfriend. I just sit here and watch daytime TV while my mum fusses around me trying to hide her tears. [*Starts crying*]

MARK: Oh, no, don't do that, oh... I'm not a tear expert... I'm not good at this, look, don't tell anyone I hugged a bloke right? Come on, come here. [*Hugs* DAVID, *then slowly exits*]

DAVID: These are my days now. Short of breath, constant diarrhoea – pretty crappy really. Going upstairs is a marathon. Leah thinks I'm making it all up, keeps wanting to take me for walks. Walks. That's a word I won't have much use for soon. I'm so scared, and then I take it out on everyone around me. Mum was fussing round and I told her to eff off. I don't mean it, I don't. I've tried everything – vitamins, meditation, positive thinking, all the treatments on offer. When the nights get dark, I just pray. And still I get sicker.

Blackout.

Scene 12

Spotlight on LEAH. DAVID *shuffling in background.*
LEAH, *writing in journal*:

> 2 July 1993. It was the tiredness. He started walking everywhere really slowly, a geriatric puffer by the age of 20. We could have got him a zimmer frame. The flu thing was terrifying. It developed into pneumonia and next thing he was rushed off to hospital. PCP. Pneumocystis Carinii Pneumonia, what a mouthful. It could kill me trying to say it.

CHORUS *enter.*

1:	Leah is confused
2:	Mum and Dad see that Time
3:	Has got the nursery rhyme
4:	Completely wrong.
5:	The old should die
6:	Before the young

7:	That is the way
8:	The song should be sung.

MARK *wheels bed on to stage with* DAVID *on it. He's hooked up to a drip on a stand.* LEAH *looks up from her writing, goes over to lay her hand on his forehead.*

LEAH:	My brother lies on his bed in his room.
	The bed is his room, his life.
	He no longer understands the verb 'to get up'.
	And outside, it rains a warm, summer rain,
	The streets now smooth as skin. [*Strokes his face*]

CHORUS *take over performance text, with movements of nurses taking temperatures, rolling* DAVID *on to his side, bringing bedpans etc.*

1:	A child,
2:	A twenty-year-old child,
3:	Curled up, hugging the duvet,
4:	Drifting gently into and out of this roaring life.
5:	Fed with food he has not cooked, mashed up in his mouth
6:	With meals of medicine to make him drowsy and
ALL:	[*Whisper*] Falling to dreams.
7:	My brother, my wonder lad.
	His lust frowned on by me,
	The righteous sister.

8:          And now, no lust, just the eyes of a boy,

            Looking out from a face that is not rosy

            Nor full cheeked,

9:          But filled with hollow places. [CHORUS *exit*]

MARK *is fussing about the bed, propping up a very weak* DAVID.
LEAH, *writing in journal*:

            25 July 1993. It's as if someone came with an

            ice-cream scoop and hollowed him out. They're

            feeding him baby food. It's so humiliating. He's

            very dehydrated. Only yesterday, he stopped being

            able to suck with a straw. Lack of liquid, that's

            what will do it, according to the nurse. At least

            he's at home now...

LEAH: Mark, could you fill up that beaker for me?

MARK: Just water, right?

LEAH: Yeah. And the nurse is having a break. Would you

            mind doing the bedpan?

MARK: No probs. Nothing I like better than a brimming

            bed pan. [*Grins*]

LEAH: You're a pal, Mark.

MARK: [*Carrying bedpan*] Well I just love taking the...

            Anyhow... he's my pal, isn't he? Though I am

            missing far more important things, like the

            football...

LEAH: Ahhhhh! [*Carries on writing*]

MUM *and* DAD *enter.*

LEAH: Hey, Mum. Hey, Dad.

DAD: Hey, David, I got that comfy pillow for you. And
          when I was rooting around, I found some of your
          soft toys from when you were a kid. Mr Bunny's
          totally legless these days, so don't encourage his
          drinking, right?

DAVID: Mmm.

DAD: Hello, Mark. Thanks for helping out. Bedpan duty,
          huh? Hi, Leah. Catching up on the diary?

LEAH: Yeah.

DAD: I wish I had a way of putting all my feelings down.

MUM: You've got me.

DAD: I've got you and Leah and David. What more could
          I ask for?

MUM: I knew it wasn't the career you wanted for him,
          but at least he's had a bash at it.

DAD: How could I have thought it wasn't a proper job?
          I was a typical Dad. But he went for his dream.
          [*Pauses and smiles*] I hope it's not too late to say
          I'm the proudest father in the world.

MUM: [*Goes over to sit on bed*] How you doin',
          masterchef?

DAVID: [*Drowsy*] Thirsty. [*He is very ill, hardly moving. She
          lifts a squeezy bottle to his lips*] Not long now,
          Mum.

MUM: Do you remember when you were little and you were always asking for a back scratch before bed? Those were the best of times. Bedtime story, cuddles and you coming to me in the night if you were scared. Now you're the brave one... my little angelcake... [*Stroking head*] For some reason, I keep thinking of that time when we all drove to Scotland in the Mini. The milk spilled, literally, stank out the car. You were both fighting, the car broke down. Then one of you dropped the keys down the only drain for ten miles.

LEAH: Wasn't me!

DAD: Not the most relaxing holiday in the world. But I wouldn't have missed it.

LEAH: Forget the holiday, it was the Kentucky Fried Chicken on the way home that sticks in my mind. Even then you were a foody snob David, writing reports in your little book about it. Leg or breast? Nothing changes!

MUM *and* DAD *groan.* DAVID *smiles weakly.*

MUM: And you two, always at it, carrying out miniature wrestling tournaments in the back seat.

LEAH: I'll miss those fights... Guess I'd win the arm wrestle now! Shall we try it, just like the old days?

CHORUS *enter as nurses again.*

DAVID: I am not stricken with plague.

	But loaded with a life well lived.
1:	When the microphone of St Peter
	Is lifted to my lips
	I'll say it was all worthwhile,
	All, and nothing less.
2:	The feast is nearly done.
	They are clearing the plates for the next sitting.
3:	I am full up with life.
MUM:	My mother will walk me to the door.
4:	My bones,
5:	My blood,
6:	My ears,
7:	My eyes,
DAVID:	My mother who played guitar to me and scratched my back,
LEAH:	My sister who I ignored,
DAD:	My father who sometimes didn't understand,
8:	What do I know of death?
9:	What do I know of this loss,
	Except that I do not want to say
ALL:	Goodbye.

Lights fade on bed and family.

Scene 13

MUM: [*Calls from darkness*] Don't forget – baby wipes, bananas, lots of spring water...

LEAH: Yeah, yeah, yeah, I'm just a walking, talking shopping machine.

Lights up, LEAH *with shopping bags looking tired.* DANIELLA *and* JO *enter.*

JO: Hey, Leah. You look like an old bag lady. Here, I'll give you a hand. [*Takes bags off Leah*] What's happening? We missed you, the last week of term.

LEAH: I'm so tired. Dad's at work; Mum's beginning to freak. It's me holding the fort right now, with the odd bit of help from Mark... I can't do it for much longer.

DANIELLA: How's your brother? Sorry we haven't been round, it's just... you know...

LEAH: Yeah, it's the holidays and who wants to hang round with terminally ill people? Not quite as much fun as clubbing.

DANIELLA: I didn't mean that. You know I didn't. We haven't seen him in the café. What's he doing?

LEAH: Nothing. He does nothing. He just sits there, getting thinner and thinner. He's so ill now. Sometimes I wish he would just die.

JO: You don't mean that?

LEAH: I do. Yes, I do. My mum and dad have gone grey overnight. Grandad has just had to go into a nursing home and their son has come home to die. It's all the wrong way round.

DANIELLA: Class wasn't the same without you.

LEAH: Teacher's been great, but some of the others are just too much. Trying not to touch me in the corridor, like I've got spikes coming out of me. Elaine avoids me as much as possible. You find out who your friends are…

CHORUS *surround* LEAH *calling* David, David, David… *Friends dissolve away, walking backwards. Chant continues as performance text starts.*

1:        A friend was calling him
          In a voice familiar as dreams.

2:        Time to go,
          To leave the room of his house,
          The four small walls of his days.

3:        Outside, the trees were singing to him,

4:        Leaf-songs,

5:        Elegies of wind,

6:        As he stepped out, cradling his death, like a lullaby.

During poem, DAVID *rises from his bed and begins slowly to walk away. He kisses his father and mother on the forehead and hugs* LEAH, *then moves off. Blackout.*

Scene 14

Lights up on family at stage left and David *at stage right, staring straight ahead.* Chorus *are holding large, long white sheet across stage, with* David *at far end. After each line of the poem, he stands and is rolled from one side of the stage to the other, like a mummy.*

1:	Bright was the sun-lidded thirteenth August day you died.
2:	My mother prayed to close your looking eyes, could not
3:	Stop the way they stared askew. Gasping, she tried [Mum *closes eyes*]
4:	To fit the face with one she knew. Then, she
5:	Cried. For this still life can never hide
6:	The deal your illness made. You lost,
7:	Much more than a pound of flesh,
8:	Breath for bone, skin to hide,
9:	Perfect skeleton
10:	With arms of string,
Leah:	What knots have You un- Tied?

Body falls on side wrapped up like mummy, carried off by Chorus. *Blackout.*

Scene 15

Leah, *writing in journal*:

> 31 August 1993. Two and a half weeks since…
> Death. The five-letter swear word. David could
> hardly speak by the end. Got really dehydrated, all
> skin and bone apart from a big pot belly. Horrible,
> but it reminded me of those pictures of the Jews in
> the camps at the end of the war. Oh well, he had
> style. Friday the thirteenth has got to be the day to
> go, if you're going to go. I just feel numb.
> Nothing. One minute he's there. The next minute,
> strange blokes with rubber gloves and a body bag
> have zipped him up and he's gone. It's too much.
> I found his leather jacket in the cupboard and put
> it on and it was way too big for me, but it smelled
> of his smell and that's when I cried and cried, by
> myself, no one to see me. Funny how my boyfriend
> hasn't been round much recently… I picked up a
> paper the other day and some nutter was ranting
> on about how AIDS was the punishment of God.
> I could almost hear him frothing at the mouth. I'd
> have loved him to come and sit with David for the
> last couple of days. Maybe then, he wouldn't be so
> judgemental.

MUM *and* DAD *come onstage, mime.*

1:	Half the world's gone mental,
2:	About the facts they seem quite vague,
3:	Calling it a gay plague!
4:	Too thick to know it runs the course,
5:	Through any kind of intercourse.
6:	But this is one family's grief,
7:	The pain is almost beyond belief.

Scene 16

LEAH, *writing in journal:*

> September 1993. Just started college. Still the same old people. You would not believe how little they say.

CHORUS *enter with* JO, DANIELLA *and* ELAINE, *and set up chairs and tables, mime being pupils.*

JO:	All right, Leah?
LEAH:	No. I mean, yes. I don't know.
DANIELLA:	Work'll take your mind off it.
LEAH:	Something like that. [ELAINE *enters*] All right, Elaine?
ELAINE:	Yeah, sorry about your brother. Hey how's it going with Matt what's-his-face?
LEAH:	History lesson.
ELAINE:	So you never, you know…

LEAH: Never what, Elaine? Never screwed him? Is that plain enough? Funnily enough, I haven't been in the mood recently… You still don't get it, do you? How safe is your current, number 26, is it? Ever heard of a condom?

ELAINE: David was just unlucky. I'm more choosy.

LEAH: That's what you think. Just hope it doesn't choose you. Now I'd like to spend some time with my real friends.

ELAINE: But I *am* your friend.

LEAH: You're infected, Elaine… with prejudice. I wish you well in your recovery. Goodbye.

ELAINE *exits.*

CHORUS *begin arranging chairs and tables to make café. Girl from* CHORUS *narrates at side of stage as* CHORUS *act out lines.*

GIRL: I'll fit you into verse with skilful ease,
Politely asked, mime the right words to say –
Be strong! Carry on! It's all in a day!
Tie up each feeling, the British disease,
Ignore my heart as it grieves, as it grieves.
Soon, a smile, like the moon comes, shining ray,
My friends shout out, 'Onwards we go!' as they
Ignore my heart and it grieves, and it grieves.

But there comes a time, I just cannot contain

It, this stone, hell-heaviness of my tears

Now brims, burns me to bear this bawling pain

I did not ask for, and it is so plain

You were not planned like rhyme. Then, what is

clear,

My brother lies dead, this poem in vain.

Scene 17

Café. Chorus *come to life.*

Leah, *writing in journal:*

> 13 August 1994. One year since David died. So this
> is grief. Just empty. The words pour out, but the
> cup is empty. [*Pours from an empty teapot*] Excuse
> me [*Hand up*] another pot of tea, please?

Mark *enters.*

MARK: Your mum said I might find you here.

LEAH: Hi, Mark.

MARK: Not the same without him, is it?

LEAH: Nope.

MARK: I've er… got this video – Aliens. Weird stuff
happens. Bad monster. Sexy heroine saves
everyone. And… your mum's at home trying one
of David's recipes – what do you reckon? A good

night in or what?

LEAH: Not in the mood, but thanks, Mark. Maybe
          another time.

MARK: Oh... right then. Well... see ya!

LEAH: Yeah. See ya... [MARK *exits*] Here is the hangout.
          The place of a thousand bits of gossip, fog of fag
          smoke, the lung cancer's day-dream. New staff,
          crap food. Time passing. So many people dying,
          but I've got my own epidemic of sadness to cope
          with. Writing sometimes helps. Setting it all down
          on paper. There it is in front of me. Somehow, I get
          a bit closer to him that way...

CHORUS *narrate poem with choreographed movements, using*
hands and faces, while remaining seated in café.

1:        Photographs remind me of your face,
          Blurring at my edges, you are out of place

2:        The key-ring my mother carries is yours,
          Though you are turning keys in different doors;

3:        Your pots and pans now cook our dinner,
          Memories of you, like soup, grow thinner.

4:        When you first died,
          Your presence was so close.
          Sometimes, I would be on the bus

5:        And there you were!
          Right next to me

In the seat, slap-bang in that moment

6: With your crazy smile

And leather jacket I was always jealous of.

7: It was a thumbs-up to my life,

The brotherly encouragement I always craved.

8: A year has gone.

You stayed for a while,

Hovering, uncertain, like an angel,

Checking up on little sister

Making sure she was OK.

9: I have to say goodbye

And if you get this letter

Let me know how you are keeping.

LEAH: Love you, brother – Leah.

DAVID *enters.*

DAVID: I got your letter.

LEAH: David.

DAVID: Leah. How's Mum and Dad?

LEAH: Yeah, just about on top of things. Can you believe it, Dad's finally left his job? You remember, he was always a big rock fan, well, he's set up a website – fossil-finding tours, hotels, the lot. 'Malachite Moments – click here to get your rocks off!'

DAVID: He's doing what he dreamed of.

LEAH: Dreaming… Mum's not so good. Sits in your room a lot. Dad's trying to interest her in the new business. She needs something since...

DAVID: What about you, little Leah?

LEAH: I miss you so much. I've got my journal. It all goes in there. I showed a couple of the poems to my teacher and she suggested I think about some writing courses. Pretty exciting really. I'm lonely... Daniella and Jo have been good mates. And Elaine? You discover who your friends are.

DAVID *nods.*

LEAH: After you... I chucked Matt for being a right insensitive git who was only after one thing. Your mate Mark misses you.

DAVID: Yeah.

LEAH: How about you, brother?

DAVID: Me.

LEAH: You. I don't suppose you can tell me much. But can I just ask one thing? Is the food any good up there?

DAVID *and* LEAH *freeze facing each other.*

CHORUS *line up, girls on one side, boys on the other.*

BOYS: Think of this,

GIRLS: I think of you,

ALL: Dream.

BOYS: We may be close

GIRLS:	Am closer now
BOYS:	As close as air
GIRLS:	As close as touch
BOYS:	Or blood or earth
GIRLS:	Or thought or breath
BOYS:	Are.
GIRLS:	Were.
BOYS:	We are one
GIRLS:	We have won.
BOYS:	By nature
GIRLS:	Despite death
BOYS:	Of all nature.
GIRLS:	All of death.
BOYS:	What we give
GIRLS:	What we lived
BOYS:	Or lose
GIRLS:	Or loved.
BOYS:	Is not given,
GIRLS:	Was not left
ALL:	Lost,
BOYS:	Just is.
GIRLS:	Just was.
BOYS:	Your brilliant eyes
GIRLS:	Your blazing words
BOYS:	Now
GIRLS:	Flow.

BOYS:	My words
GIRLS:	My crying eyes
BOYS:	Now
GIRLS:	Flow
BOYS:	Far.
ALL:	That's all.

Lights fade.

The End

PLAYS WITH ATTITUDE

REHEARSAL IDEAS

Plus suggestions for follow-up discussion suitable for PHSE.

Discussion

1 Fact and fiction: The play is set in the early 1990s, well before the advent of anti-retroviral drugs in the West. At this time, AIDS was a terminal and inescapable condition. Discuss and list what facts you know about HIV and AIDS. Discuss what sort of myths there are about the virus, particularly about how it is contracted. Make a list under the headings: True/Untrue.

2 Most of us have experienced loss and grief at some point in our lives. Our response to personal tragedy varies enormously according to personality, circumstance and feeling. The news that someone close to us is facing a potentially terminal illness or pain or trauma of any kind carries its own personal threat to our sense of well-being. Our reactions can range from anger, devastation, shock, numbness, bitterness or even guilt. There is no 'right' way to feel. Discuss the range of feelings and reactions expressed throughout this play or in a particular section. What is your own immediate response either to the play as a whole or the section considered?

3 Read the poems which are to be performed by the chorus on p19 and p31. These are extracts, written by Mark Peters, who died of AIDS in 1993. How does this information affect your response to these two pieces? Does this knowledge affect your personal performance of these sections? If so, how?

Role-play

1 In groups, choose one person to take on the role of Leah. Ask her questions about her feelings and reactions. The person playing Leah should answer in character, basing replies partly on information in the text and partly on personal response to 'How would I feel in Leah's position?' Do the same for David and for David's friend, Mark. Give feedback on what difficulties this exercise presents to the person in role.

2 In pairs, role-play the following situation: *A* has just heard that his/her brother/sister/friend has been diagnosed either as being terminally ill or as being HIV positive (remember that now, with combination therapy, being HIV positive is no longer necessarily terminal). *B* is *A*'s friend who listens, asks questions and responds in any way appropriate to the situation. In groups, discuss and compare the different responses of the *A*s to the news and how the *B*s reacted.

Improvisation

1 There are significant time jumps in Leah's journal which mean we don't see some of the situations referred to. Improvise the scene where David, with Leah's support, tells his parents what has happened to him.

Character Development

1 In role as David, write and perform a monologue about waiting for the results.

2 In role as Leah, write and perform a monologue, based on the poem on p51/52 (narrated by girl from chorus).

Performing the text

1 The poetic chorus sequences often have minimal stage directions to allow for experimentation with the most effective way of performing them. These sections are intended to be very visual in effect and suit being carefully choreographed. A good way of finding interesting stage pictures is to work initially to create a series of linked tableaux (freeze-frames) e.g. for p19 'These are the silent days'. Why are they the silent days? What sort of

atmosphere do you want to create visually? Try creating seven tableaux for each line of 'Leave it' on p31. Create six tableaux for 'For when my brother dies' on p25.

2   You can also think about how to create atmosphere using voice and group chanting. Look at the chorus section on p47: 'A friend was calling him...' Experiment with group choral sound effects, to be performed as the lines are spoken. Try different whispering sounds or words repeated with soft rhythms. Evaluate effect.

3   All the chorus lines have been divided up for a chorus group of 10. However, the chorus can be any size, according to the number of performers. In small groups of between four and six, experiment with different ways of chopping up and allocating chorus lines. Comment on the effect.

ABOUT THE AUTHORS

Andrew Fusek Peters is an author, performer and playwright with many years' experience in education. His plays include *The Wild* – a promenade play with a cast of a hundred teenagers. His TV credits include BBC1's *Wham Bam Strawberry Jam*, *Carlton Country*, *Heart of the Country* and *Mark Owen's Celebrity Scooters*.
Find out more at www.tallpoet.com

Polly Peters is a drama teacher, youth and community theatre director and writer. Her published plays include *Czech Tales* and *The Mullah Nasrudin*.

Andrew Fusek Peters and Polly Peters are the original 'been there, done that' writers. Their plays grab themes such as peer pressure, relationships, bullying, drinking and drugs and don't let go until they're finished.
Together, they have written thirty plays, anthologies, and storybooks, including the bestselling, critically acclaimed teenage collection for Hodder Wayland
– *Poems with Attitude*:

'… bursting with the raw emotion and hormone-fuelled experimentation of youth … It is rare and welcome to find a collection that speaks so directly to teenagers'
– *The Guardian*

'I cannot emphasise how much every school needs this'
– *The School Librarian*.

'Gems that make you think about real issues'
– *Daily Telegraph*

ABOUT THE CONSULTANT

Pauline Sidey Lisowska has taught English and Drama in schools and colleges throughout the UK. An author, editor and theatre director, she has also worked as a consultant for the BBC. She is currently producing a film and directing poetry shows in London's West End.

PLAYS WITH ATTITUDE

If you've enjoyed 'Angelcake', try these other titles in the series:

Dragon Chaser

It's 1981. Punk is all the rage, Charles and Diana are getting married and drugs are in. A group of friends experience the ups and downs of experimentation. On their quest for the ultimate trip, one of them will trip up badly!

Suitable for Key Stage 4 and above

Much Ado About Clubbing

A normal Saturday night out turns into a series of hysterical cheesy chat-ups, Olympic tongue-training sessions and embarrassing drunken moments, when a group of wannabe Casanovas and flighty flirts hit the town for some serious action.

Suitable for Key Stage 3/4

Twisted

Only one thing is certain: a girl is in a coma. How she got there and what actually happened is a mystery. As the plot thickens, expect the unexpected. Who is the real victim here?

Suitable for Key Stage 3/4

You can buy all these books from your local bookseller, or order them direct from the publisher. For more information about *Plays with Attitude*, write to: *The Sales Department, Hodder Children's Books, a division of Hodder Headline Limited, 338 Euston Road, London, NW1 3BH.*